Collins
INTERNATIONAL
PRIMARY

Wellbeing

Student's Book 4

William Collins' dream of knowledge for all began with the publication of his first book in 1819.

A self-educated mill worker, he not only enriched millions of lives, but also founded a flourishing publishing house. Today, staying true to this spirit, Collins books are packed with inspiration, innovation and practical expertise.

They place you at the centre of a world of possibility and give you exactly what you need to explore it.

Collins. Freedom to teach.

Published by Collins

An imprint of HarperCollins*Publishers*
The News Building, 1 London Bridge Street, London,
SE1 9GF, UK

HarperCollins*Publishers*
Macken House, 39/40 Mayor Street Upper, Dublin 1 D01 C9W8

Browse the complete Collins catalogue at
collins.co.uk

British Library Cataloguing-in-Publication Data
A catalogue record for this publication is available from the British Library.

Cambridge International copyright material in this publication is reproduced under licence and remains the intellectual property of Cambridge Assessment International Education.

Third-party websites and resources referred to in this publication have not been endorsed by Cambridge International Education.

Endorsement indicates that a resource has passed Cambridge International Education's rigorous quality-assurance process and is suitable to support the delivery of a Cambridge curriculum framework. However, endorsed resources are not the only suitable materials available to support teaching and learning, and are not essential to achieve the qualification. Resource lists found on the Cambridge website will include this resource and other endorsed resources.

Any example answers to questions taken from past question papers, practice questions, accompanying marks and mark schemes included in this resource have been written by the authors and are for guidance only. They do not replicate examination papers. In examinations the way marks are awarded may be different. Any references to assessment and/or assessment preparation are the publisher's interpretation of the curriculum framework requirements. Examiners will not use endorsed resources as a source of material for any assessment set by Cambridge International Education.

While the publishers have made every attempt to ensure that advice on the qualification and its assessment is accurate, the official curriculum framework, specimen assessment materials and any associated assessment guidance materials produced by the awarding body are the only authoritative source of information and should always be referred to for definitive guidance.

Our approach is to provide teachers with access to a wide range of high-quality resources that suit different styles and types of teaching and learning.

For more information about the endorsement process, please visit www.cambridgeinternational.org/endorsed-resources

Series editors: Kate Daniels and Victoria Pugh
Authors: Kate Daniels and Victoria Pugh
Publisher: Elaine Higgleton
Product Manager: Cathy Martin
Product developer: Roisin Leahy
Development and copy editor: Jo Kemp
Proofreader: Claire Throp
Permissions researcher: Rachel Thorne
Illustrations: Jouve India Ltd.
Cover designer: Amparo Barrera, Kneath Associates and Gordon MacGilp
Typesetter: Sam Vail, Ken Vail Graphic Design
Production controller: Sarah Hovell
Printed and bound by Martins the Printers

MIX
Paper | Supporting responsible forestry
FSC™ C007454

This book is produced from independently certified FSC™ paper to ensure responsible forest management.

For more information visit: www.harpercollins.co.uk/green

Access and download editable versions of these resources and the accompanying PowerPoint presentations at collins.co.uk/internationalresources

We are grateful to the following teachers for providing feedback on the resources as they were developed:
Ms Hema Gehani and Ms Seema Desai at Colours Innovation Academy, Ms Manjari Tennakoon and Ms Surani Maithripala at Gateway Colleges, and Preeti Roychoudhury, Farishta Dastur Mukerji, Spriha Patronobis and Sukonna Halder at Calcutta International School.

Contents

Hello and welcome to Wellbeing Stage 4's student's book!

Feelings are important

When you can talk about how you feel it is easier for other people to help you. It also helps you feel calmer and less confused.

You will be able to practise understanding and naming your feelings throughout this workbook.

It will help you learn to get on better with other people like friends or family. And it will also help you cope when things change.

Keep practising

We look after our bodies with good food and exercise, and we need to look after our minds too. That's what the activities in this book will help you do. They will help you feel more confident about yourself.

Practice makes everything easier. So, when you learn new things from this book it's a good idea to have a go at them in real life.

Self-care

As you work through this workbook you will learn some brilliant ways to take care of yourself when things feel difficult or when you try something new.

It's lovely when other people look after you and help you, but it is even better when you can do that for yourself. It's important to have some tools up your sleeve to care for yourself and know what to do when you are finding things difficult. We call that self-care.

Are you ready to learn all about it?

May your year ahead be as FANTASTIC as you are!

– *Becky Goddard-Hill*

Unit 4.1 Emotions

What do you know?

- What emotions do you know about?
- How do you know when you feel happy or sad?

In this unit, you will:

- Explore a range of emotion words and what they mean.
- Look at ways that your body might react when you feel different emotions.
- Discuss what it means to be resilient and reflect on your own experiences.

Lesson 1 What are emotions?

Activity 1.1a Matching emotions

Match the emotion words in the word bank to each of the pictures below.
Write the correct word on the line for that picture.

> excited   shy   confused   angry   happy   scared   sad   nervous

_____

_____

_____

_____

Lesson 1 What are emotions?

Activity 1.1b Reflection

Choose two emotions (e.g. happy, excited) and reflect on a time when you have felt that way. You might like to share these examples with your talking partner. You can choose any emotion to reflect on.

I felt _____

when _____

_____

_____

_____

_____

_____

I felt _____

when _____

_____

_____

_____

_____

_____

_____

_____

Lesson 1 What are emotions?

Activity 1.1c Emotion log

Today I felt _____

_____

_____

Today I felt _____

_____

_____

Today I felt _____

_____

_____

Today I felt _____

_____

_____

Today I felt _____

_____

_____

Today I felt _____

_____

_____

Today I felt _____

_____

_____

Lesson 2 How does my body react?

Activity 1.2a How might my body react?

Match the emotion in the left column with the physical effect it has on the body in the right column, using the examples at the bottom of the page. If you would like to share, you can put an example of when you have felt that way in the My example column.

Can you think of any other emotions and give some examples of physical effects in the empty boxes?

Emotion	Physical effect	My example
Happiness		
Fear or feeling scared		
Anger		
Sadness		

slumped posture

slow movements

tearful eyes

clenched jaw

raised voice

increased heart rate

sweating

tense muscles

smiling

relaxed muscles

feeling light

Lesson 2 How does my body react?

Activity 1.2b Emotion story

Write a paragraph to describe how Anu might be feeling. Remember to mention the way her body is responding and how she might be feeling physically.

_____

_____

_____

_____

_____

_____

_____

_____

You can illustrate the story with a picture below.

Unit reflection

In the bubbles, write your own reflections for each question.

1. What are emotions?

2. Think of a time when you have experienced a strong emotion. How did your body react?

3. Think of a time when you have been resilient. How did you feel at the time?

Unit 4.2 Managing my emotions

Emotion wheel

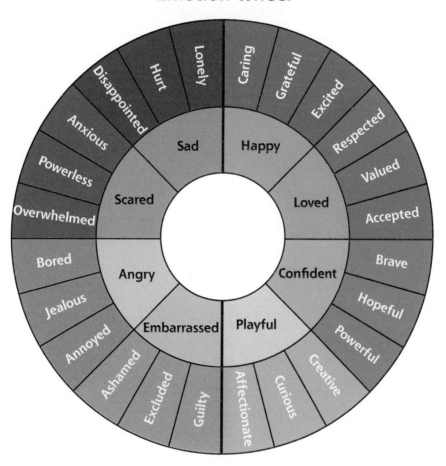

What do you know?

- Look at the emotion wheel. Are there any emotion words that are new to you?
- Choose one word from the outer wheel. Can you use it in a sentence?

In this unit, you will:

- Explore triggers for different emotions.
- Consider when behaviour is appropriate to a situation and what to do if it isn't.

Lesson 1 Why do I feel this way?

Activity 2.1 Emotion storyboard

Choose one of the scenarios from the lesson and consider how each character might react to the situation. What emotions might they be feeling? Create a storyboard with words or pictures of what might happen next.

Lesson 2 Runaway thoughts

Activity 2.2a And Now Nobody Likes Me

How does Carrie feel in the story so far? Have you ever felt this way?

_____

_____

_____

_____

How does Carrie feel when she is finishing her work in the classroom?

_____

_____

_____

_____

What might Carrie be feeling as she gets outside?

_____

_____

_____

_____

What do you think might happen next in the story?

_____

_____

_____

_____

Lesson 2 Runaway thoughts

Activity 2.2b How to manage your thoughts

Read the information below. Have you tried any of these strategies?

What other ways could Carrie manage her emotions in this situation? What might help?

Annotate the information below with your own ideas, words or pictures to show other strategies to manage your emotions.

What can help?

Don't compare yourself to others

The key is to focus on yourself. Can you improve how you did last time in the spelling test, or can you make a new friend? Turn your envy into a goal instead.

Think it through

If you think, rather than just feel, you can put your jealousy into perspective.

You will recall that when you were younger, you got all the attention because babies are helpless and need a lot of care.

You will remember that you have other friends who you can invite to sleepovers too.

Don't fear missing out

Fear of missing out can make you jealous, so get rid of the fear by focusing on the good things in your life.

Maybe it's time to invite a new friend home for a meal or visit a family member?

Be a cheerleader

Say "well done" to the classmate who beat you in the test, ask your best friend how the sleepover went and offer to help out with the new baby. Don't give in to your jealousy; instead make your relationships happier and stronger.

– Becky Goddard-Hill

13

Lesson 2 Runaway thoughts

Activity 2.2c Managing my emotions

Consider strategies that might be helpful if you or a friend are having runaway thoughts. Write or draw the strategies in the trainer below.

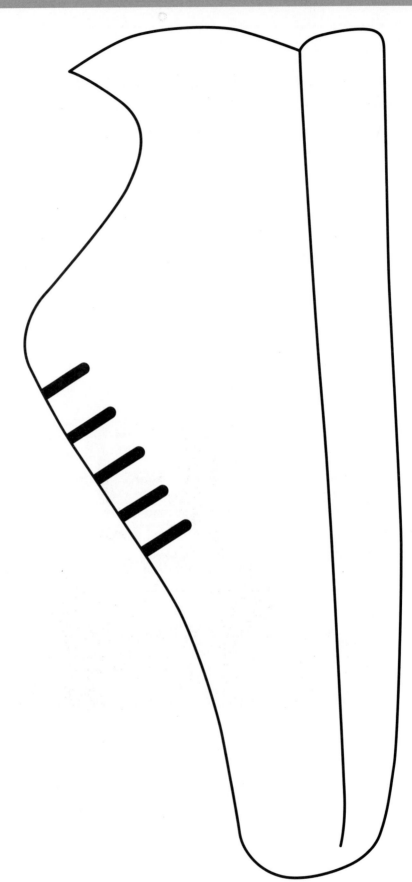

Lesson 3 Looking after my mind

Activity 2.3 Time to relax

Think of all the ways you like to relax. Reflect on these below. What are your favourite ways to relax? Why? What else would you like to try?

Unit reflection

Consider times when you feel particular emotions. Are they primary or secondary emotions? You can use the emotion wheel to help you decide.

Write five sentences below to show some triggers for your emotions.

For example, 'When I am lonely, I feel sad.'

Emotion wheel

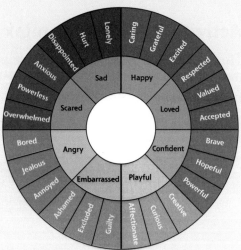

1. _____

_____

2. _____

_____

3. _____

_____

4. _____

_____

5. _____

_____

What strategies might you use to manage these emotions?

What do you know?

- What is happening in the photo?
- Have you had a similar experience to the photo?
- What does the term "healthy lifestyle" mean?
- What does "hygiene" mean?

In this unit, you will:

- Explore a range of ways to keep your body and mind healthy.
- Describe ways to ensure good oral hygiene.
- Create a balanced diet and identify key food groups.

Lesson 1 Creating a balanced meal

Activity 3.1a What do I like?

Try as many of the foods as possible. Consider how they look, taste and feel. Which foods did you enjoy?

Food	Add notes about how the food tastes or feels	Do you like it? 😊 or ☹

Lesson 1 Creating a balanced meal

Activity 3.1b Which food group does it belong to?

Look at your daily menu you wrote on Worksheet 4.3.1a. Using the information on pages 20–21, pick out the key ingredients and colour-code each one to show which food group it belongs to:

blue for protein – **red for dairy** – **green for fruit and vegetables**

yellow for fats and sugars – orange for starchy carbohydrates

---

My menu

Breakfast

Key ingredients

Lunch

Key ingredients

Dinner

Key ingredients

Lesson 1 Creating a balanced meal

Activity 3.1c Nutrition information

A balanced diet helps to ensure that our body and mind receives a wide variety of vitamins, minerals and proteins. Read the information below to help you work out which food groups the foods in your menu contain. Can you make your menu even more balanced?

What foods do you enjoy from each food group?

Nutrients for a healthy mind and body

Starchy carbohydrates are a type of food that can give us lots of energy to play and have fun! They can be found in foods like potatoes, bread, rice and pasta. These foods are important because they provide our bodies with the fuel we need to run, jump, and play all day long. Starchy carbohydrates are also a good source of fibre, which helps keep us full and our digestion healthy.

Proteins are essential for a healthy body, especially for growing children. They are important for building and repairing muscles, bones and other tissues. They also help to make enzymes, hormones and other chemicals that are needed for good health. Foods that are rich in protein include meat, fish, eggs, beans, nuts, and dairy products like milk and cheese. It is important to eat a variety of protein-rich foods to get all the different types of proteins that your body needs.

Dairy products, such as milk, cheese and yogurt, are an important part of a healthy and balanced diet. They are rich in calcium, which helps to build strong bones and teeth. They also contain other important nutrients like vitamin D, which helps the body absorb calcium, and vitamin B12, which is important for the nervous system. They also provide protein, which is essential for growth and development.

Fruits and vegetables are packed with nutrients that help our bodies work properly, like vitamins, minerals and fibre. They can also help protect our bodies from getting sick by boosting our immune system. Eating a variety of colours is important too, because different coloured fruits and vegetables have different nutrients. For example, orange fruits are rich in vitamin C, which helps our skin heal and fight off infections.

Some fats, like those found in nuts, seeds and oily fish, are necessary for our bodies to function properly. These healthy fats provide energy, help absorb vitamins, and protect vital organs.

Sugars, on the other hand, should be consumed in moderation, as they can cause tooth decay. Natural sugars in fruits and dairy products are a better option than added sugars found in processed foods and drinks.

Lesson 2 Looking after your oral health

Activity 3.2a Looking after my teeth

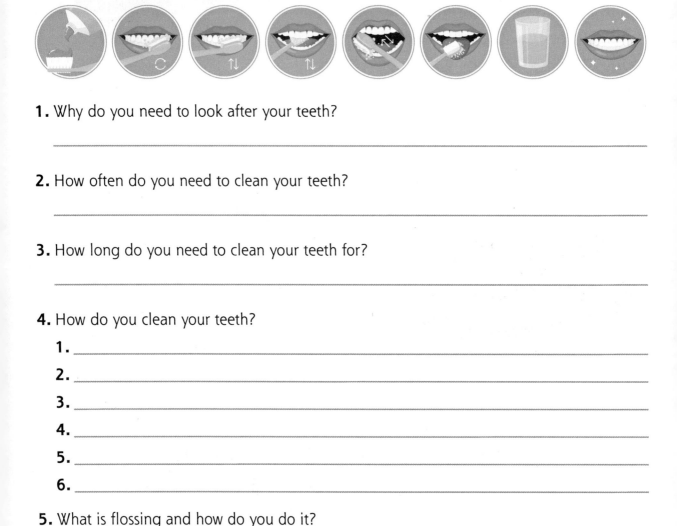

1. Why do you need to look after your teeth?

_____

2. How often do you need to clean your teeth?

_____

3. How long do you need to clean your teeth for?

_____

4. How do you clean your teeth?

    1. _____

    2. _____

    3. _____

    4. _____

    5. _____

    6. _____

5. What is flossing and how do you do it?

_____

_____

6. What have you learned about how your diet can affect your teeth?

_____

_____

_____

_____

Lesson 2 Looking after your oral health

Activity 3.2b My teeth and mouth

Add labels to each part of the mouth and teeth in the diagram below.

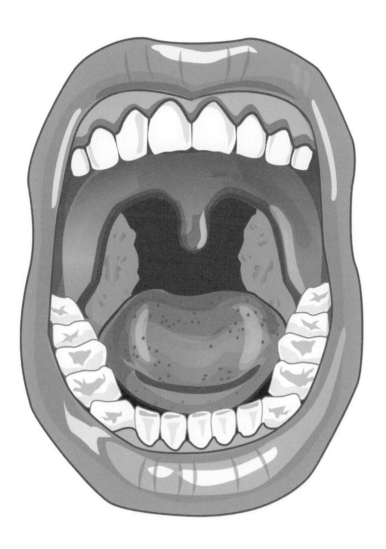

Unit reflection

Create a colourful poster which reminds other children how to keep clean and healthy. You can include all aspects of health you have learned about in this unit. You can include words and phrases too.

What do you know?

- What do you know about relationships?
- Why do you think friendships are important?

In this unit, you will:

- Learn about different types of relationships.
- Find out why friendships are so important.
- Explore whether something fun could actually be bullying.

Lesson 1 All the people I know

Activity 4.1a Different relationships

Today you are learning about relationships. How many different relationships can you think of? Write them down, creating a web from the word 'relationships'. Don't worry, this isn't a test! It's for your teacher to see what you know.

Lesson 1 All the people I know

Activity 4.1b Reflection

Think quietly about what you have learned about different relationships in your life.

Use this page to write or draw what you think and what you have learned.

Is there anything more you would like to know or don't understand about relationships? Write your questions here and your teacher can answer these for you.

Lesson 2 Good friends

Activity 4.2a Different types of friends

Today you are learning about friendships. How many different types of friends can we have? Write down as many as you can think of, creating a web from the word 'friendships'. Don't worry, this isn't a test! It's for your teacher to see what you know.

Lesson 2 Good friends

Activity 4.2b Reflection

Think quietly about what you have learned about what makes a fantastic friend.

Use this page to sketch what you and your friends drew as a fantastic friend – you can label it too. Now think quietly about what you might like to introduce into your friendships following this lesson.

Is there anything more you would like to know about friendships? Write your questions here and your teacher can answer these for you.

_____

_____

Is there anything worrying you about friendships?

_____

_____

Lesson 3 It's only a joke!

Activity 4.3a Top five ways to help

How could you help when you see someone being teased or someone being mean to another person? Write down your top five ideas.

1. _____
_____
_____

2. _____
_____
_____

3. _____
_____
_____

4. _____
_____
_____

5. _____
_____
_____

Lesson 3 It's only a joke!

Activity 4.3b Acrostic poem

How do you think we should treat each other in our school to show respect for everyone? Arrange your ideas in an acrostic poem below. (An acrostic is a poem where each letter of a word is used to start a new line of the poem.)

R _____

_____

E _____

_____

S _____

_____

P _____

_____

E _____

_____

C _____

_____

T _____

_____

Unit reflection

You have been asked to collect information about different relationships for a time capsule in your town. You can look back at the introduction to this unit to help you think about where you started.

Complete the sheet below to go in the time capsule with all the information you have learned.

Name: _____   Date: _____

Subject: *Everything I know about relationships* _____

_____

_____

_____

_____

_____

_____

_____

_____

_____

_____

_____

_____

_____

_____

_____

_____

_____

_____

_____

_____

_____

Unit 4.5 Respect

What do you know?

- What can you see in the picture?
- Do you know what these mean?
- Why might they be used?

In this unit, you will:

- Create a rules collage.
- Hold a class debate.
- Practise your active listening skills.

Lesson 1 Rules, rules, rules

Activity 5.1 Choose the rules

Choose some rules which you have in your class or home. What could be the consequences if people didn't follow these rules?

1. *The rule*

If we ignored this rule the consequences might be

2. *The rule*

If we ignored this rule the consequences might be

3. *The rule*

If we ignored this rule the consequences might be

Lesson 2 Different opinions

Activity 5.2a Debating points

Write your key points for the debate below. Remember to make them clear and concise.

- My key argument:

- Key point 1:

- Key point 2:

- Key point 3:

- Concluding point:

Lesson 2 Different opinions

Activity 5.2b Reflect on the debate

What did you find useful about the debate? What did you find less useful?

_____

_____

_____

Did it change your opinion?

_____

_____

_____

Was it difficult to give your opinions when others disagree?

_____

_____

_____

What have you learned?

_____

_____

_____

Lesson 2 Different opinions

Activity 5.2c Voicing your opinion respectfully

Write or draw three ways in which you can voice your opinion in a respectful way when you don't agree with others.

I can use my voice to...

I can be respectful by...

When I want to share my opinion, I can...

Lesson 3 Are you a good listener?

Activity 5.3a Listener's checklist

Your name: _____

Student being observed: _____

Area to observe	Outcome	Notes
Shows positive body language (leans forward and has an open manner)		
Empathises (tries to see the situation from the other person's side)		
Listens actively without interrupting		
Asks open questions		
Encourages the other person to solve their own problems		
Did they say any of these? Please circle if they did.		Tell me about… How do you feel about… On a scale of 1–10… What would you like to change? What could you do to solve this problem? What can I do to help you? I see…/Yes…/I understand… That must be hard for you. If you could wake up tomorrow and find that this problem had gone away, how would everything be different?

Lesson 3 Are you a good listener?

Activity 5.3b Being a good listener

Can you think of all the ways that being a good listener might help you in your life now and in the future? Draw or write your reflections below.

How will good listening skills help me in my life?

Unit reflection

What does respect mean to you?

Draw or write your ideas below.

How do you show respect to others?

_____

_____

_____

_____

Write three things you have learned from this unit.

1. _____

_____

2. _____

_____

3. _____

_____

Unit 4.6 Keeping safe

What do you know?

- What hazards can you see in the photos?
- Why do you think there are rules, regulations and restrictions online?

In this unit, you will:

- Think about how to keep safe in your day-to-day life.
- Learn about different hazards and how to keep safe.
- Think about how to stay safe online.

Lesson 1 Keeping safe around strangers

Activity 6.1a Thinking about keeping safe

You are going to be learning about keeping safe in this unit.

Let's see what you know about this subject already. List all the ways that you keep yourself safe. This can be at home, at school or out in public. How many different situations can you think of? Write these down below.

Lesson 1 Keeping safe around strangers

Activity 6.1b Places I go

Sketch a simple map of all the places you go in one week. These places might include: home, school, sports pitch, club, shops, parents'/carers' workplaces, friends' houses, playground, park, countryside.

Lesson 2 Managing hazards

Activity 6.2 Thinking about hazards

1. Stick your 'spot the hazard' photo here.

2. List the hazards that you have added in your picture.

_____

_____

_____

3. If you were in this place, what would you do to keep yourself safe? Think about everything you have learned in this lesson and write down below what you would do, or not do, to keep safe in this place.

_____

_____

_____

_____

_____

Lesson 3 Keeping safe online

Activity 6.3a True or false

There are lots of potential harms on the internet, but there are also lots of simple things we can do online to keep ourselves safe.

Go through the true/false statements below. If you're not sure what the answer is, just go with what you think it probably is. This is not a test! It is to help you learn, and to help your teacher to support you to keep safe online.

Statement	True or false?
Only be friends with people who you know in real life.	
Always be kind online.	
Ignore age restrictions: use any website or game for any age.	
Never share any private information online (e.g. name, address, school, phone number).	
Believe everything you read and see online.	
Share and show your parents/carers anything you are worried about online.	
Never click on any pop-ups or attachments.	
Set simple passwords.	
Never pretend to be older than you are.	
Report anything suspicious. Get an adult you trust to help you.	

Go through the answers with your teacher, then answer these questions.

1. Are there any statements in the table that you had never thought of before or that you do not understand? Write them here so that your teacher can help you with them.

_____

_____

_____

_____

_____

2. Is there anything you are learning about today that is worrying you? If so, talk to an adult you trust and they can help you. Write your worry below.

_____

_____

_____

_____

_____

Lesson 3 Keeping safe online

Activity 6.3b Reflection

Add some bullet points below about what you have learned about online safety.

Is there anything you need to do or learn more about? (Please include as much detail as you can so that your teacher can help you.)

Do you need help with anything from a trusted adult? If so, can you explain what help you would like?

If you are worried about anything you have learned in this lesson, make sure you talk to an adult you trust so that they can help you.

Unit reflection

Thinking about the hazards and dangers you have been learning about, draw a picture of yourself putting the safety measures covered in this unit in place.

How many can you add? You can circle these safety measures and label them if you feel this will make them clearer.

Unit 4.7 Changes

What do you know?

- What do you know about the value of mistakes?
- What do you think 'thinking about your thinking' means?

In this unit, you will:

- Explore changing friendships.
- Consider how, from different perspectives, mistakes may not be all they seem.
- Learn how to watch your thoughts.

Lesson 1 When friendships change

Activity 7.1 What I have learned

Use this Venn diagram to consider all that you have learned about how to deal with changes and disagreements in relationships.

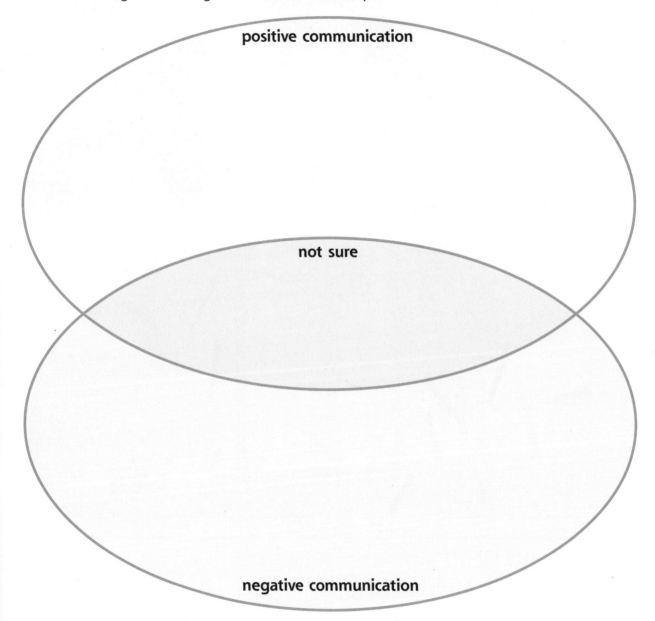

Write down one strategy which you feel would be useful in the future when dealing with friendship disagreements, and one strategy for how to seek help and get the support you need when friendships change.

1. _____

2. _____

Lesson 2 Mistakes

Activity 7.2a What I think of mistakes...

Write or doodle your thoughts about mistakes on this page.

For example, what do you think of others making mistakes? What do you think of yourself when you make mistakes? Do you think mistakes are good or bad or both? Why?

Lesson 2 Mistakes!

Activity 7.2b Leo's story

Leo was an artist who lived high up in a little village in the hills.

Along with growing vegetables, he had sketched and drawn with pencils since he was a little boy.

He loved to watch the sky, the moon and the sun, the shadows and the seasons. He always noticed things around him, often little things that other people did not.

The villagers would come to him to ask if he could draw a picture for them to send to a relative far away.

'He's so talented,' they would say.

This was the way it was and the way it had always been with Leo, but one evening as he was tidying up his little home, he realised that every single picture he had ever drawn was grey. It hit him, just like that!

He looked out of his window and noticed, as he always did, all the beautiful colours around him and suddenly, just like that, he made a promise to himself that from now on he was going to use colour – he was going to learn to paint!

The very next day, he set off to the nearest town and returned with brushes and canvases and with tubes of paint in every colour you could imagine!

He set straight to work, sitting on the edge of his field overlooking the valley. He painted the sky and the trees and the people working in their fields, the birds, the flowers, on and on.

Finally, as the light was fading, he stepped back from his work to see how it looked … and it looked AWFUL!

None of the colours looked real; there were brushstrokes and paint runs.

When the villagers saw it, they all said, 'Oh dear! He's made a big mistake; he should stick to what he's good at.'

But Leo would not give up. Every day he went out and painted and painted and painted. But he didn't feel happy with his work.

One evening, a friend came to see him and Leo told him about his mistake – the money and time he had wasted at something he would never be good at.

'I'll just go back to drawing,' he said. 'I know I can do that.'

'Wait, let me see your work,' said his friend.

When he saw it he was amazed. 'This is incredible, Leo!'

'Don't tease me!' said Leo.

'No, I mean it! Your work is unique and intriguing. I love it! You need to change your perspective. Your mistake is a gift – for where there is grey, you now have colour!'

Answer these questions, thinking back to
Leo's story.

1. Why do you think the villagers thought Leo
had made a mistake?

_____

_____

_____

_____

_____

2. Why did Leo think he had made a mistake?

_____

_____

_____

3. What did Leo's friend see that everyone else hadn't?

_____

_____

_____

4. Do you think Leo made a mistake or not? Why?

_____

_____

_____

5. How can this story help you to think more positively about your
mistakes?

_____

_____

_____

Lesson 3 Think about your thinking

Activity 7.3a

Try thinking about your thinking with these questions.

1. When does your brain do its best thinking?

_____

_____

_____

2. What helps you?

_____

_____

_____

3. How do you manage your thinking?

_____

_____

_____

Lesson 3 Think about your thinking

Activity 7.3b Visualisation

In this lesson you were taught the basic skills of relaxation. This visualisation builds on that technique to help us to support our thinking.

Sit comfortably with your back straight against the chair, with both feet on the ground, your hands on your lap and your eyes gently closed.

Become aware of sitting in your chair and then take your awareness to your breathing – notice how air goes in and out of your body. Listen to this and feel it go in and out.

Breathe comfortably and slowly and count your breath in and out.

Thoughts might come into your head. If this happens or your mind wanders, simply bring your thinking back to your breathing.

Now imagine a television screen in front of you. On the screen you can see a bright blue sky on a sunny day.

There are fluffy white clouds floating across the sky and the air is warm.

You feel really calm and happy.

You realise that all the fluffy clouds are your thoughts and if you listen really carefully you might even be able to hear them.

Whether you hear your thoughts or not, just let them drift past you on the clouds and float away across the blue sky and off the screen.

Watch the clouds float past for a while, seeing your thoughts come and go.

When you feel ready, open your eyes and have a good stretch.

Reflection on the visualisation

How did that visualisation feel?

What did you notice about your thoughts?

Was there anything you really liked about it?

Was there anything you found hard?

Unit reflection

Friendship issues, making mistakes and thinking can all be hard work! Can you list one thing from each lesson that you are going to practise? Write them down here.

1. _____

2. _____

3. _____

Sometimes it's good to find a way to relax and switch off our thinking and our actions and simply enjoy 'being' and finding our calm centre.

Here is a visualisation for you to learn. Once you have got the hang of this, you can use it any time to calm your mind and centre yourself.

A feeling of calm

Your mind is very powerful, and your imagination has the power to help you relax.

Think about the feelings in your body right now – are any of your muscles tense or uncomfortable? Think about each part of your body. Start at the top of your head and scan down over your face, your torso, your arms and legs, all the way to your toes.

As you breathe in, imagine you are breathing in the feeling of calm.

As you breathe out, imagine you are breathing out any feelings of tension or anxiety.

– Poppy O'Neill

Unit 4.8 One world

What do you know?

● What does this Indigenous American proverb mean to you?

*We do not inherit the earth from our ancestors (people who came before us).
We borrow it from our children.*

In this unit, you will:

● Learn about the 4 Rs.

● Take a look at some of the issues around plastic pollution.

● Understand the 30 human rights.

Lesson 8.1 Reduce, recycle, reuse, repurpose

Activity 8.1 Planning a persuasive letter

Write a letter to your headteacher or school governors, explaining the importance of the 4 Rs: Reduce, Recycle, Reuse, Repurpose. Think about how best to explain what the terms mean, give examples of ways in which the school can encourage them and point out the benefits to the school and the environment. Plan the key points you want to include in each section.

Introduction

_____

_____

Reduce

_____

_____

Recycle

_____

_____

Reuse

_____

_____

Repurpose

_____

_____

Conclusion

_____

_____

Lesson 8.2 How does plastic affect our planet?

Activity 8.2a My pledge

In these images we see what happens when we use plastic bottles once and don't recycle. What can you do to change this?

We all have the power to make change for the better…

I pledge _____

_____

_____

_____

Lesson 8.2 How does plastic affect our planet?

Activity 8.2b Plastic and our planet

Read this information about plastics to learn more and then answer the questions.

All about plastic

Plastic is made using oil, gas or coal. Scientists discovered how to make the first plastics in the nineteenth century.

Plastics are a very versatile material which has become widely used for a huge variety of purposes due to it being waterproof, flexible, adaptable and cheap to make.

The biggest drawback, however, is the cost to the planet. Plastic is not biodegradable, which means that it cannot be broken down naturally and will take centuries to break up and disappear.

Plastic can end up in rivers, the sea and other waterways, causing pollution and danger to wildlife, which can get caught up in it or eat it by mistake.

Because it doesn't biodegrade, it can float in the sea for many years and get carried around the globe by the sea's currents. As a result, there are now huge patches of plastic floating in the some of the world's oceans.

1. Why are plastics so popular?

_____

_____

_____

_____

_____

2. What is the main drawback of plastic?

_____

_____

_____

_____

_____

Lesson 8.3 Human rights

Activity 8.3 The 30 human rights

Read the information below to learn about the 30 different human rights.
An article is a separate paragraph or note outlining one of the rules.

Article 1	Article 2	Article 3
Everyone is born free and deserves equal rights.	Everyone has basic human rights regardless of their differences.	Everyone has the right to live, be free, and be safe.
Article 4	**Article 5**	**Article 6**
No one should be held as a slave.	No one should be tortured or be treated as less than human.	Everyone has the right to be recognised as a person no matter where they are.
Article 7	**Article 8**	**Article 9**
Everyone should be treated as equal by the law.	The law should protect anyone whose rights have been violated.	No one should be arrested, placed in prison or exiled without a legitimate reason.
Article 10	**Article 11**	**Article 12**
Everyone has the right to a fair trial by a fair court.	Everyone should be considered innocent until they are proven guilty of a crime. Penalties must be fair.	Everyone has the right to privacy and their reputation.
Article 13	**Article 14**	**Article 15**
Everyone has the right to travel freely.	Everyone can escape to another country if they are seeking asylum from persecution in their country.	Everyone has the right to choose and maintain the country of their nationality.
Article 16	**Article 17**	**Article 18**
Everyone has the right to get married and build a family. Both partners have equal rights.	Everyone has the right to own property. No one should have their property taken away without reason.	Everyone has the right to choose or change their religious beliefs.

Article 19 Everyone has the right to express their opinion and to receive information through any media.	**Article 20** Everyone has the right to assemble peacefully.	**Article 21** Everyone has the right to participate in their government and elect officials.
Article 22 All members of society have a right to social security.	**Article 23** Everyone has the right to fair working conditions, fair salary, equal pay for equal work, and the right to form and join trade unions.	**Article 24** Everyone has the right to reasonable work hours, including periodic holidays with pay and the right to rest and leisure.
Article 25 Everyone has the right to adequate living conditions, food, health care, and security in the event of circumstances beyond their control.	**Article 26** Everyone has the right to a good education.	**Article 27** Everyone has the right to participate in community cultural activities and to share in scientific advancements.
Article 28 Everyone is entitled to a society in which the rights and freedoms of this declaration can be fully realised.	**Article 29** It is our responsibility to protect the rights of others.	**Article 30** Your human rights can never be taken away.

Which human right, or human rights, do you think are most important and why?

_____

_____

_____

_____

_____

_____

Unit reflection

Consider what you have learned across this unit. Write or draw your new knowledge below.

What are the three most interesting things you have learned?

1. _____

   _____

2. _____

   _____

3. _____

   _____

Do you have any questions or anything else you now want to learn more about?

_____

_____

_____

Acknowledgements

We are grateful to the following for permission to reproduce copyright material:

4.1.3. Cover image from *The Thing Lou Couldn't Do* written and illustrated by Ashley Spires, cover illustration © 2017 Ashley Spires. Reproduced by permission of Kids Can Press Ltd., Toronto. **5.4.3**, An extract about bullying, NSPCC, https://www.nspcc.org.uk/what-is-child-abuse/types-of-abuse/bullying-and-cyberbullying/. Reproduced with permission; **5.6.3**, "Game age ratings explained", PEGI, copyright © PEGI S.A. Reproduced with permission; and **5.7.2**, Quotes by Sir James Dyson, https://www.dyson.com/james-dyson, copyright © Sir James Dyson, 2011-2023. Reproduced with kind permission.

The Publishers wish to thank the following for permission to reproduce images and copyright material. Every effort has been made to trace copyright holders and to obtain their permission for the use of copyright materials. The publishers will gladly receive any information enabling them to rectify any error or omission at the first opportunity.

4.1.1 SB p. 1 (tl) Vector bucket/ Shutterstock, (tr) StudioBrandShop/ Shutterstock, 4.1.1 (hl) ober-art / Shutterstock, (br) Vector bucket/ Shutterstock, 4.1.1 PPT Slide 1 MillaF/Shutterstock, Slide 3 & SB p. 2 jsabirova/Shutterstock, Slide 4 violetkaipa/Shutterstock, Slide 5 Yury Zap/ Shutterstock, WS 4.1.1a jsabirova/Shutterstock, **4.1.2** PPT Slide 1 Ground Picture/ Shutterstock, Slide 2 (l) PeopleImages.com – Yuri A/ Shutterstock, (tr) Roman Samborskyi/ Shutterstock, (br) anut21ng Stock/ Shutterstock, Slide 3 Gelpi/Shutterstock, Slide 4 YASH GARG FOTOGRAFIE/ Shutterstock, WS 4.1.2b YASH GARG FOTOGRAFIE/ Shutterstock, **4.1.3** PPT Slide 1 & SB p. 8 MinskDesign/ Shutterstock, Slide 2 Cover image from The Thing Lou Couldn't Do written and illustrated by Ashley Spires, cover illustration © 2017 Ashley Spires. Reproduced by permission of Kids Can Press Ltd., Toronto. **4.2.1** PPT Slide 5 Oleg Nesterov/ Shutterstock, Slides 1-5 Reprinted by permission of HarperCollins Publishers Ltd © 2023, Lisa Rajan, **4.2.2** Ealita.ID/ Shutterstock, SB p14 Ealita.ID/ Shutterstock, SB p. 15 Nicoleta Ionescu/Shutterstock, **4.2.3** WS Nicoleta Ionescu/ Shutterstock, PPT Slide 1 Iconic Bestiary/ Shutterstock, Slide 2 (tl) Moosavefoto/ Shutterstock, (t) Monkey Business Images/ Shutterstock, (tr) Africa Studio/ Shutterstock, (bl) Shyamalamuralinath/ Shutterstock, (br) Jacob Lund/ Shutterstock, Slide 3 (tl) Patrick Foto/Shutterstock, (tr) Elena Yakusheva/Shutterstock, (bl) Govind Jangvir/Shutterstock, (br) Daria Medvedeva/Shutterstock, **4.3.1** WS 4.3.1a Jr images/ Shutterstock, SB p. 17 RomanR/ Shutterstock, PPT Slide 1 Tatjana Baibakova/ Shutterstock, Slide 3 Kaspars Grinvalds/ Shutterstock, Slide 7 & SB pp20–21 NIPAPORN PANYACHAROEN/ Shutterstock, Slide 7 & SB pp20–21 MarcoFood/ Shutterstock, Slide 7 & SB pp20–21 Tim UR/ Shutterstock, Slide 7 & SB pp20–21 Ermak Oksana/ Shutterstock, Slide 7 & SB pp20–21 Dionisvera/ Shutterstock, Slide 7 & SB pp20–21 baibaz/ Shutterstock, Slide 7 & SB pp20–21 Craevschii Family/ Shutterstock, Slide 7 & SB pp20–21 New Africa/ Shutterstock, **4.3.2** PPT Slide 1 (r) Daxiao Productions/ Shutterstock, (l) RomanR/ Shutterstock, Slide 2 & SB p. 23 Benjamin Ordaz/ Shutterstock, Slides 3 & 6 inspiring.team/ Shutterstock, SB 4.3.2 inspiring.team/ Shutterstock, **4.3.3** PPT Slide 1 (b) Riccardo Mayer/ Shutterstock, (tl) PeopleImages.com – Yuri A/ Shutterstock, (tr) aslysun/ Shutterstock, Slide 3 Ory Gonian/ Shutterstock, Slide 4 riopatuca/ Shutterstock, Slide 6 yusufdemirci/ Shutterstock, **4.4.1** SB p. 25 (t) Monkey Business Images/Shutterstock, p. 25 (r) Rohit Seth/Shutterstock, p. 25 (b) Monkey Business Images/Shutterstock, p. 26 Athanasia Nomikou/ Shutterstock, **4.4.2** SB p. 28 Athanasia Nomikou/ Shutterstock, WS 4.4.2 Athanasia Nomikou/ Shutterstock, PPT Slide 1 (tl) Sophon Nawit/ Shutterstock, (tr) Rawpixel.com/ Shutterstock, (bl) Denis Kuvaev/ Shutterstock, (br) Ground Picture/ Shutterstock, Slide 2 wavebreakmedia/ Shutterstock, Slide 3 (tl) Prostock-studio/ Shutterstock, (t) Ground Picture/ Shutterstock, (tr) mguttman/ Shutterstock, (bl) Darrin Henry/ Shutterstock, (b) Monkey Business Images/ Shutterstock, (bl) Reshetnikov_art/ Shutterstock, Slide 4 Monkey Business Images/ Shutterstock, **4.4.3** PPT Slides 1 & 2 Rawpixel.com/ Shutterstock, slides 3 & 4 Lemberg Vector studio/ Shutterstock, Slide 5 Dmitry Demidovich / Shutterstock, Slide 6 theshots.co/ Shutterstock, SB p. 32 Svetliy/ Shutterstock, **4.5.1** SB p. 33 (tl) dzejdi/ Shutterstock, (tr) IZZ HAZEL/ Shutterstock, (bl) nikolae/ Shutterstock, (br) TotemArt/ Shutterstock, PPT Slide 4 Ken Cook/ Shutterstock, **4.5.2** PPT Slide 3 ESB Professional/ Shutterstock, Slide 4 & SB p. 36 OlyaOK/ Shutterstock, pp. 37 & 40 Eightshot_Studio / Shutterstock, SB Eightshot_Studio / Shutterstock, **4.5.3** PPT Slide 1 (br) Africa Studio/Adobe Stock, (tr) ilikestudio/ Shutterstock, (bl) vesna cvorovic / Shutterstock, (tl) UfaBizPhoto/ Shutterstock, Slide 2 Littlekidmoment/ Shutterstock, Slide 3 Elena_Dig / Shutterstock, Slide 4 & SB p. 39 Luis Molinero/ Shutterstock, Slide 5 Thinglass / Shutterstock, Slide 6 New Africa / Shutterstock, **4.6.1** SB p41 (tl) cunaplus/ Shutterstock, (tr) Dinesh Hukmani/ Shutterstock, (bl) Fedor Selivanov/ Shutterstock, (br) Motortion Films/ Shutterstock, PPT Slide 1 Kirk Fisher/ Shutterstock, Slides 2 & 5 Gina Kelly / Alamy Stock Photo, **4.6.2** PPT Slide 1 (tl) nik_nadal/ Shutterstock, (tr) ADM Photo / Shutterstock, (bl) fotokaleinar / Shutterstock, (br) vchal / Shutterstock, Slide 2 mindscanner/ Shutterstock, **4.6.3** SB p. 46 hurricanehank/ Shutterstock, WS 4.6.3 hurricanehank/ Shutterstock, PPT Slide 1 Prostock-studio/ Shutterstock, Slide 2 Prostock-studio / Shutterstock, Slide 4 Monkey Business Images / Shutterstock, **4.7.1** SB p. 49 & PPT 4.7.2 Slide 1 (tr) Roman Samborskyi/ Shutterstock, 4.7.1 SB pp. 49 & 54, ChristianChan / Shutterstock, SB p. 49& 4.7.1 PPT Slide 1 imtmphoto / Shutterstock, 4.7.1 PPT Slide 2 Erik Clegg / Shutterstock, 4.7.1 PPT Slide 3 WESTOCK PRODUCTIONS / Shutterstock, 4.7.1 PPT Slide 4 designkida / Shutterstock, 4.7.1 PPT Slide 5 Nach-Noth / Shutterstock, **4.7.2** PPT Slide 1 (l) ChristianChan / Shutterstock, (br) Dina Belenko/ Shutterstock, Slide 2 & SB p. 53 Zainudin_Kho / Shutterstock, WS 4.7.2 Zainudin_Kho / Shutterstock, **4.7.3** PPT Slide 1 Prostock-studio/ Shutterstock,

Slide 2 boxstock / Shutterstock, **4.8.1** SB p. 57 max dallocco/ Shutterstock, PPT slide 1 Preres/ Shutterstock, slide 2 Prapat Aowsakorn/ Shutterstock, slide 3 Studio_G/ Shutterstock, SB p. 58, PPT, WS Studio_G/ Shutterstock, **4.8.2** PPT slide 1 & SB p59 © HarperCollins Publisher 2020, slides 2 & 3 (tl) AlenKadr/ Shutterstock, slides 2 & 3 (tr) Teerasak Ladnongkhun/ Shutterstock, slides 2 & 3 (bl) Mike Truchon/ Shutterstock 4.8.2 (br) M88/ Shutterstock, slide 5 Part of Design/ Shutterstock, SB p. 60 (t) frank60/ Shutterstock, (b) Rich Carey/ Shutterstock, SB p. 61 Maryshot/ Shutterstock, **4.8.3** PPT Slide 1 Lightspring/ Shutterstock, **5.1.1** SB p. 1 (tl) Atomic Roderick/ Shutterstock, (tr) Jasmine Creation/ Shutterstock, (b) mentalmind/ Shutterstock, PPT Slide 1 asiandelight/ Shutterstock, Slide 2 Michael Kraus/ Shutterstock, **5.1.2** PPT Slide 1 (l) Sabrina Bracher/ Shutterstock, (r) Queenmoonlite Studio/ Shutterstock, Slide 2 Natalie Board/ Shutterstock, Slide 3 Andrekart Photography/ Shutterstock, Slide 4 Chay_Tee/ Shutterstock, Slide 5 © HarperCollins Publishers 2020, **5.1.3** SB p.6 HowLettery/Shutterstock, p.7 CallMeTak/ Shutterstock WS HowLettery/Shutterstock, PPT Slide 1 Rambleron/Vecteezy, Slide 2 (t) Ground Picture/ Shutterstock, (bl) Godong/ Alamy Stock Photo, (br) James Kirkikis/ Shutterstock, Slide 3 Microstocker.Pro/ Shutterstock, Slide 4 GoodStudio/ Shutterstock, Slide 4 TALVA/ Shutterstock, **5.2.1** SB p.9 KlingSup/ Shutterstock, PPT Slide 1 Kolonko/ Shutterstock, Slide 2 metamorworks/ Shutterstock, Slide 3 Ground Picture/ Shutterstock, Slide 4 (tl) minizen/ Shutterstock, (t) Net Vector/ Shutterstock, (tr) giedre vaitekune/ Shutterstock, (bl) Yuri Chuprakov/ Shutterstock, (b) Simakova Mariia/ Shutterstock, (br) backUp/ Shutterstock, **5.2.2** PPT Slide 1 Kaspars Grinvalds/Shutterstock, Slide 2 Vladimir Gjorgiev/ Shutterstock, Slide 3 Africa Studio/ Shutterstock, Slide 4 Mariia Boiko/ Shutterstock, Slide 5 Nor Gal/ Shutterstock, SB p.13 karakotsya/ Shutterstock, **5.2.3** PPT Slide 1 (l) & SB p.16 Viktorija Reuta/ Shutterstock, Slide 1 (r) maglyvi/ Shutterstock, Slide 2 & 3 Daisy Daisy/ Shutterstock, Slide 2 + 3 Timolina/ Shutterstock, Slide 2 + 3 Hung Chung Chih/ Shutterstock, Slide 2 + 3 alif_Osman/ Shutterstock, Slide 2 + 3 ESB Professional/ Shutterstock, Slide 3 Wahyu Ananda/ Shutterstock, Slide 3 wavebreakmedia/ Shutterstock, Slide 4 (l) stockpexel/ Shutterstock, (r) wavebreakmedia/ Shutterstock, Slide 4 PeopleImages.com – Yuri A/ Shutterstock, SB p.15 (l) Aleksandr Merg/ Shutterstock, WS 5.2.3a Aleksandr Merg/ Shutterstock, SB p. 15 (r) woocat/ Shutterstock, WS 5.2.3a woocat/ Shutterstock, WS 5.2.3b, SB p.16 Viktorija Reuta/Shutterstock, **5.3.1** SB p.17 (tl) pixelheadphoto digitalskillet/ Shutterstock, (tr) F01 PHOTO/ Shutterstock, (b) fizkes/ Shutterstock, PPT Slide 1 (l) fizkes/ Shutterstock, (r) Nowaczyk/ Shutterstock, Slide 2 (l) SeventyFour/ Shutterstock, (r) Solid photos/ Shutterstock, Slide 3 (tl) fizkes/ Shutterstock, (r) Krakenimages.com/ Shutterstock, (bl) MalikNalik/ Shutterstock, SB p.18 (t) & PPT Slide 4 PixyPen/ Shutterstock, TG WS PixyPen/ Shutterstock, SB p.18 (b) Colorfuel Studio/ Shutterstock, TG WS Colorfuel Studio/ Shutterstock, **5.3.2** PPT Slide 1 ANURAK PONGPATIMET/ Shutterstock, Slide 2 + 3 (bl) Lakmal Ditmax/ Shutterstock, PPT Slide 2 (tr) Lapina/ Shutterstock, Slide 2 (br) New Africa/ Shutterstock, Slide 3 (t) Carkhe/ Shutterstock, (l) Kolonko/ Shutterstock, TG WS 5.3.2, **5.3.3** PPT Slide 1 (b) WEB-DESIGN/ Shutterstock, Slide 3 Studio Barcelona/ Shutterstock, Slide 5 Frenggo/ Shutterstock, PPT Slide 6 katsuba_art/Shutterstock, **5.4.1** SB p.25 Rawpixel.com/ Shutterstock, p.26 Vegorus/ Shutterstock, WS Vegorus/ Shutterstock,SB p.27 Monkey Business Images/ Shutterstock, PPT Slide 1 (tl) IndianFaces/ Shutterstock, (tr) SALMONNEGRO-STOCK/ Shutterstock, (bl) Aleem Zahid Khan/ Shutterstock, (br) Yuri Dondish/ Shutterstock, Slide 3 wellphoto/ Shutterstock, **5.4.2** PPT Slide 1 & SB p.29 afry_harvy/ Shutterstock, Slide 2 Pressmaster/ Shutterstock, Slide 3 LightField Studios/ Shutterstock, SB p.30 Reprinted by permission of HarperCollins Publishers Ltd © 2022 A. M. Dassu, **5.4.3** PPT Slides 4–6 Intellson/ Shutterstock, **5.5.1** SB p.33 SewCreamStudio/ Shutterstock, PPT Slide 2 (tl) Prostock-studio/ Shutterstock, (tr) HAKINMHAN/ Shutterstock, (bl) Image bug/ Shutterstock, (br) pixelheadphoto digitalskillet/ Shutterstock, Slide 3 vectornation/ Shutterstock, Slide 4 Pixel-Shot/ Shutterstock, **5.5.2** PPT Slide 1 (tl) memej/ Shutterstock, (t) Yukhym Turkin/ Shutterstock, (tr) Aletkina Olga/ Shutterstock, (bl) Glinskaja Olga/ Shutterstock, (br) woocat/Shutterstock, Slide 2 Sudowoodo/ Shutterstock, Slide 4 MARI_NAD/ Shutterstock, **5.5.3** PPT Slide 1 & SB p.37 Elena Zajchikova/ Shutterstock, Slide 2 tangguhpro/ Shutterstock, Slide 3 Seqoya/ Shutterstock, Slide 4 & SB p.38 Victoria 1/ Shutterstock, SB p.38 Maksym Drozd/ Shutterstock, **5.6.1** SB p.41 WESTOCK PRODUCTIONS/ Shutterstock, PPT Slide 3 & SB p.42 Pungu x/ Shutterstock, WS Pungu x/ Shutterstock, PPT Slide 5 Pixel-Shot/ Shutterstock, Slide 6 Roman Arbuzov/ Shutterstock, **5.6.2** SB p.45 (t) TR STOK/ Shutterstock, (b) Gatien GREGORI/ Shutterstock, SB p.45 Text Reprinted by permission of HarperCollins Publishers Ltd © 2022 Mio Debnam, PPT Slide 1 trgrowth/ Shutterstock, Slide 2 Phonix_a Pk.sarote/ Shutterstock, Slide 3 Pakhnyushchy/ Shutterstock, Slide 4 kornnphoto/ Shutterstock, Slide 5 Dmitry Naumov/ Shutterstock, Slide 6 AntiD/ Shutterstock, **5.6.3** SB p.47 Reprinted by permission of HarperCollins Publishers Ltd © 2023 Jo Cotterill, SB p.48 (t) Monster Ztudio/ Shutterstock, (l) Rafael Croonen/ Shutterstock, (b) Luce Altra/ Shutterstock, PPT Slide 1 SynthEx/ Shutterstock, Slide 2 HamaVision/Shutterstock, Slide 3 (tr) smx12/Shutterstock, (r) Oleksandra Klestova/ Shutterstock, (br) Toxa2x2/ Shutterstock, Slide 4 Aleksandra Suzi/ Shutterstock, **5.7.1** SB pp. 49&56 Darkdiamond67/ Shutterstock, PPT Slide 1 Food Impressions/ Shutterstock, Slide 3 winyuu/ Shutterstock, Slide 4 Petar Dojranliev/ Shutterstock, **5.7.2** SB p.53 GoodStudio/ Shutterstock, PPT Slide 1 Olena Yakobchuk/ Shutterstock, Slide 3 (tl) Winai Tepsuttinun/ Shutterstock, (t) Elnur/ Shutterstock, (l) luchschenF/ Shutterstock, (t) rvlsoft/ Shutterstock, (c) Passakorn sakulphan/ Shutterstock, (r) Ilina Yuliia/ Shutterstock, (tr) Sergio33/ Shutterstock, (bl) Volodymyr Krasyuk/ Shutterstock, (b) Pixel-Shot/ Shutterstock, (br) Chonlatee42/ Shutterstock, Slide 4 horst friedrichs / Alamy Stock Photo, **5.7.3** PPT Slide 1 ImageFlow/ Shutterstock, Slide 4 Serhii Bobyk/ Shutterstock, Slide 5 Red Fox studio/ Shutterstock, **5.8.1** SB p.57 nexus 7/ Shutterstock, p.58 piotr_pabijan/ Shutterstock, p59 &

PPT Slide 1 MintBlac/ Shutterstock, Slide 2 checy/ Shutterstock, Slide 3 Monster Ztudio/ Shutterstock, Slide 4 (tr) rtbilder/ Shutterstock, (l) Ugis Riba/ Shutterstock, (br) Pakphoom9/ Shutterstock, **5.8.2** SB p.60 & PPT Slide 1 Shane Gross/ Shutterstock, Slide 2 Elime/ Shutterstock, **5.8.3** SB p.62 BearFotos/ Shutterstock, WS BearFotos/ Shutterstock, PPT Slide 1 (t) Paolo Bona/ Shutterstock, (bl) Dani Vincek/ Shutterstock (br) Tae PY15MU/ Shutterstock, Slide 2 (t) WitR/ Shutterstock, (bl) Melnikov Dmitriy/ Shutterstock, (br) aphotostory/ Shutterstock, Slide 3 & SB p. 64 Dmitrijs Mihejevs/ Shutterstock, Slide 5 (l) Johny Bayu Fitantra/ Shutterstock, (r) j.chizhe/ Shutterstock, **6.1.1** SB p.1 F01 PHOTO/ Shutterstock, p.2 Asti Mak/ Shutterstock, p.3 (t) Roman Samborskyi/ Shutterstock, (b) Prostock-studio/ Shutterstock, PPT Slide 1 Marish/ Shutterstock, Slide 3 & SB p.7 Dmytro Onopko/ Shutterstock, Slide 4 (l) marekuliasz/ Shutterstock, (tr) Ronnachai Palas/ Shutterstock, (tb) CREATISTA/ Shutterstock, **6.1.2** SB p.5 (t) JPC-PROD/ Shutterstock, (b) Veja/ Shutterstock, PPT Slide 1 Text Reprinted by permission of HarperCollins Publishers Ltd © 2023 Kathryn Kendall Boucher, Slide 1 S K Chavan/ Shutterstock, Slide 2 (t) Ground Picture/ Shutterstock, Slide 2 (l) Ground Picture/ Shutterstock, (r) Creativa Images/ Shutterstock, slide 3 Esteban De Armas/ Shutterstock, Slide 4 Just dance/ Shutterstock, **6.1.3** PPT Slide 1 (l) Anastasia Shilova/ Shutterstock, (tr) MIA Studio/ Shutterstock, (br) Elena Nichizhenova/ Shutterstock, Slide 2 VectorPlotnikoff/ Shutterstock, Slide 3 Nicoleta Ionescu/ Shutterstock, SB p. 7 Vector bucket/ Shutterstock, Yayayoyo/ Shutterstock, Yayayoyo/ Shutterstock, Vector bucket/ Shutterstock, Yayayoyo/ Shutterstock, Dmytro Onopko/ Shutterstock, p.8 IYIKON/ Shutterstock, **6.2.1** SB p.9 Dejan Dundjerski/ Shutterstock, PPT Slide 1 (l) pathdoc/ Shutterstock, (r) pathdoc/ Shutterstock, Slide 2 (l) imtmphoto/ Shutterstock, (r) Monkey Business Images/ Shutterstock, Slide 3 (tl) cdrin/ Shutterstock, (tr) fizkes/ Shutterstock, (bl) lovelyday12/ Shutterstock, (br) Pressmaster/ Shutterstock, Slide 4 & SB p.11 Brian A Jackson/ Shutterstock, Slide 5 &SB p.11 Arcady/ Shutterstock, Slide 6 & SB p.11 Yuganov Konstantin/ Shutterstock, **6.2.2** SB p.12 T. Lesia/ Shutterstock, PPT Slide 2 Khoroshunova Olga/ Shutterstock, Slide 4 xtock/ Shutterstock, **6.2.3** PPT Slide 1 (tl) Stock Exchange/ Shutterstock, (tr) TinnaPong/ Shutterstock, (bl) jianbing Lee/ Shutterstock, (br) vivanvu/ Shutterstock, 6.2.3PPT Slide 3 (tl) Laboo Studio/ Shutterstock, (t) matimix/ Shutterstock, (bl) wavebreakmedia/ Shutterstock, (br) Jose Gil/ Shutterstock, (tr) M Stocker/ Shutterstock, Slide 4 Pressmaster/ Shutterstock, SB p.16 (b) Zoart Studio/ Shutterstock, (t)Vitalii Petrenko/ Shutterstock, WS 6.3.1 p.129 Zoart Studio/ Shutterstock, **6.3.1** SB p.18 Zoart Studio/ Shutterstock, p.17 Jeruik/ Shutterstock, PPT Slide 3 Andrii Yalanskyi/ Shutterstock, **6.3.2** PPT Slide 1 (tl) javi_indy/ Shutterstock, (tr) Monkey Business Images/ Shutterstock, (bl) Pressmaster/ Shutterstock, (br) pixelheadphoto digitalskillet/ Shutterstock, Slide 2 & SB p. 24 Iconic Bestiary/ Shutterstock, Slide 3 German Vizulis/Shutterstock, Slide 4 Pictorial Press Ltd / Alamy Stock Photo, Slide 5 (t) Chronicle / Alamy Stock Photo, (b) Reprinted by permission of HarperCollins Publishers Ltd © 2013 Anne Rooney, SB p.21 wavebreakmedia/ Shutterstock, **6.3.3** SB p.22 UnderhilStudio/ Shutterstock, p. 23 Oxy_gen/ Shutterstock , WS 6.3.3 UnderhilStudio/ Shutterstock, PPT Slide 1 (l) Tanya Antusenok/ Shutterstock, (r) Piotr Urakau/ Shutterstock, Slides 2 &3 Fotomay/ Shutterstock, Slide 4 Natata/ Shutterstock, **6.4.1** SB pp.25&32 AMR Studio/ Shutterstock, PPT Slide 2 Colored Lights/ Shutterstock, **6.4.2** PPT Slides 2&6 Ruslana Iurchenko/ Shutterstock, Slides 3&6 (r) A Sharma/ Shutterstock, Slide 3 (l) LightField Studios/ Shutterstock, Slide 4 SynthEx/ Shutterstock, **6.4.3** PPT Slide 1 Alina Reynbakh/ Shutterstock, Slide 3 TungCheung/ Shutterstock, Slide 5 Olivier Le Moal/ Shutterstock, SB p.30 Nata Bene/ Shutterstock, **6.5.1** SB p.33 Rawpixel.com/ Shutterstock, p.34 Rudie Strummer/ Shutterstock, PPT Slide 1 Yuliya Chsherbakova/ Shutterstock, Slide 2 WESTOCK PRODUCTIONS/ Shutterstock, Slide 3 marekuliasz/ Shutterstock, **6.5.2** PPT Slide 1 (TL) Kehinde Temitope Odutayo/ Shutterstock, (tr) CHEN WS/ Shutterstock, (bl) arun sambhu mishra/ Shutterstock, (b) Free Wind 2014/ Shutterstock (br) Lewis Tse/ Shutterstock, Slide 2 (tl) ESB Professional/ Shutterstock, (tr) Daniel M Ernst/ Shutterstock, (bl) Anirut Thailand/ Shutterstock, (br) MUHAMMAD IZZAT TERMIZIE/ Shutterstock, Slide 4 (tl) Monkey Business Images/ Shutterstock, (tr) BRAIN2HANDS/ Shutterstock, (b) Evgeny Atamanenko/ Shutterstock, **6.5.3** PPT Slides 1 + 2 ssguy/ Shutterstock, Slide 3 SALMONNEGRO-STOCK/ Shutterstock, Slide 4 Ronnachai Palas/ Shutterstock, Slide 5 (tr) Sabrina Bracher/ Shutterstock, (tl) oneinchpunch/ Shutterstock, (t) Kristof Bellens/ Shutterstock, (bl) Sarawut Chamsaeng/ Shutterstock, (br) imtmphoto/ Shutterstock, Slide 7 justaa/ Shutterstock, SB p.39 Nizwa Design/ Shutterstock, **6.6.1** SB p.41 (tl) Antlii/ Shutterstock, (r) maicasaa/ Shutterstock, (bl) omphoto/ Shutterstock, SB p.42 & PPT slide 2 Vitalii Vodolazskyi/ Shutterstock, WS 6.6.1 Vitalii Vodolazskyi/ Shutterstock, PPT Slide 1 13_Phunkod/ Shutterstock, Slide 3 512r/ Shutterstock, **6.6.2** PPT Slide 1 elenabsl/ Shutterstock, Slide 2 Standard Studio/ Shutterstock, SB p.44/ PPT Slide 4 EreborMountain/Shutterstock, SB p.45 Reprinted by permission of HarperCollins Publishers Ltd © 2020 Lisa Rajan, **6.6.3** PPT Slide 1 & SB p.46 desdemona72/ Shutterstock, **6.7.1** SB p.49 Jacques Paganel/ Shutterstock, PPT Slide 1 Viacheslav Lopatin/Shutterstock, Slide 2 GoodStudio/ Shutterstock, Slide 3 &SB p. 50 (t) Vasilinka/ Shutterstock, Slide 3 & SB p.50 (b) Bibadash/ Shutterstock, SB p.51 Simakova Mariia/ Shutterstock, WS 6.7.1, **6.7.2** PPT Slide 1 Sipa/Shutterstock, Slide 3 Gustavo Frazao/ Shutterstock, **6.7.3** PPT Slide 1 Vgstockstudio/ Shutterstock, Slide 3 Gorodenkoff/ Shutterstock, SB p.56 Christina Designs/ Shutterstock, **6.8.1** SB p.57 Nostalgia for Infinity/ Shutterstock, PPT Slide 1 (tl) Ermolaev Alexander/ Shutterstock, (tr) DisobeyArt/ Shutterstock, (br) rangizzz/ Shutterstock, (bl) Diyana Dimitrova/ Shutterstock, Slide 2 Tang Yan Song/ Shutterstock, Slide 3 (tl) Marquess789/ Shutterstock, (tr) Vitalii Karas/ Shutterstock, (bl) lovelyday12/ Shutterstock, (br) Sergey Ryzhov/ Shutterstock, **6.8.2** PPT Slide 2 Thinglass/ Shutterstock, Slide 3 Photo_Pix/ Shutterstock, **6.8.3**SB p.63 Lightspring/ Shutterstock, p.64 phloxii/ Shutterstock, WS 6.8.2 Simakova Mariia/ Shutterstock